Pioneer Buildings of British Columbia

Pioneer Buildings of British Columbia

Rudi Dangelmaier

Harbour Publishing

HARBOUR PUBLISHING
P.O. Box 219
Madeira Park, BC Canada V0N 2H0

Printed and bound in Hong Kong by Colorcraft

Cover and text design by Fiona MacGregor
Edited by Hajo Hadeler

Co-published with SU Press, 1–13 Ikuta-cho I-chome, Chuo-ku, Kobe 651, Japan

Canadian Cataloguing in Publication Data

Dangelmaier, Rudi, 1909–
   Pioneer buildings of British Columbia

   ISBN 1-55017-012-0

   1. Historic buildings—British Columbia—
Pictorial works.   2. British Columbia—
Description and travel—Views.   I. Title.
FC3812.D35 1989   971.1'0022'2   C89-091431-1
F1087.8.D35 1989

Overleaf: **Fishing settlement, Lulu Island**

For my wife, Margaret, and our extended family

Friends encourage. Institutions make things possible. I gratefully acknowledge their help and assistance.

Bob Switzer
Stan Thomas
Jane (Sharpe) De Vitt
Marcel Veronesi
The Canada Council
The Union of British Columbia Indian Chiefs
The British Columbia Provincial Museum
Yvonne Klan
Don Lord

Overleaf: **Original hotel in Carmi**

Many mining towns in British Columbia were named after sites in the United States because the mines were started by Americans. "Greenwood" for example originated in Colorado, and "Carmi" in Illinois.

Today Carmi, BC, is a ghost town twenty-five miles north of Rock Creek. At the turn of the century a silver mine supported several hundred people. Like so many of its kind, the small town died when profits failed to meet expectations.

A few shacks remain, some empty houses and a few dilapidated places of business. The wind chases ghosts in the old hotel near the mining site.

Until 1950 Mrs. Muir operated a little store on the main floor. There was even a short revival in the 1940s, when various groups from Rutland and Penticton rented the place and some real parties made the dance hall ring with music and laughter. But that too is long past now.

Contents

Preface

Old buildings and structures have always held a special fascination for me. The people may have deserted them long ago, but somehow their hopes and ambitions still linger in the enduring work of their hands. Each building is also a story.

The paintings in this book represent a true labour of love. It was a joy to paint, a challenge to capture the charm, and to document what was destined to disappear. It was not possible to be comprehensive, but in my selectivity I tried to be truly representative.

What a pleasure it was for Margaret and myself to drive out into the country in search of that special site! Sometimes we wandered around for hours before we found an interesting subject. And then I couldn't wait to take out my sketch pad. When darkness fell we went home, intent on coming back soon.

Several times it happened that the house or the church simply disappeared while we were gone. Once, I remember, we returned the very next day, but the beautiful log homestead I was painting had been bulldozed into a creek overnight.

Indeed, my interest as a painter gave me a unique perspective on just how rapidly and thoughtlessly these pioneering structures—British Columbia's true folk architecture—were being swept away and forgotten. I began to realize that the paintings I had done were in many cases the only record that remained, and what had begun out of personal fascination took on the character of heritage preservation. As the collection grew to a hundred or more works, friends persuaded me that it should eventually be completed and published as a book.

The results you hold in your hands.

Rudi Dangelmaier

Foreword

Martin Segger

British Columbia has long been known through the art of its painter-documentalists. Rudi Dangelmaier maintains a tradition that includes the expedition artists who accompanied James Cook on his northwest coast voyages. Only through their eyes do we today see early Indian village life and the majesty of the first landfall sites. Similarly, British colonial administrators and would-be settlers learned of our scenic grandeur through the watercolour sketches of military surveyors, engineers and draftsmen.

During the 1840s and 50s this province's landscape was recorded by men such as Lieut. Henry James Ware, a reconnaissance officer investigating the British–United States boundary dispute and John Clayton White, a Royal Engineer who also worked his way to northern reaches of the province with the ill-fated Western Union Telegraph Company. Frederick Whymper, a professional artist and illustrator, recorded early life in the Cariboo goldfields and was artist to the Vancouver Island Expedition. The object of these artists was to document topographical features, habitations and contemporary activities. It is fascinating that Rudi Dangelmaier should revisit and portray many of those same early sites in the Fraser Valley, on the Cariboo Wagon Road and the southern Kootenays.

Dangelmaier also shares with these early documentalists a no-nonsense technical approach to his work. Military field sketching began with a pencil sketch; light colour washes were added to create perspective and highlight significant features. The work was then firmed up with pen-and-ink; extraneous pencil marks were finally erased. Yet while objectivity was a goal, works of this kind still bear the unmistakable stamp of contemporary aesthetics. Current interest in the picturesque, the topical fascination with antique ruins cultivated during a European grand tour, no doubt influenced surveyors and journalists alike to focus on the craggy canyons of the Fraser or abandoned native villages.

While photography was destined to supplant the quick surveyor's sketch as a record of the landscape moment, the scenic treasures of British Columbia have continued to maintain a vibrant tradition of landscape painting. In the early years of the 20th century, local watercolourists of the arts-and-crafts movement such as Samuel Maclure in Victoria and the reclusive Charles John Collings in the Okanagan interpreted what they saw through the hazy mists of impressionism or Japanese brush techniques. Rudi Dangelmaier prefers the earlier tradition. But often in the stylized treatment of a skyscape or the watery blending of colours in a prairie ground cover, the vision is at once romantic and impressionistic.

More than anything else however, within both the tradition of the romantic ruin and the technical approach of the military field sketch, these works pass comment on the architectural evidence of British Columbia growing up. Our architectural history of pioneer homesteads and gold-rush boomtowns is fleeting and ephemeral. Sketches such as Fraser Valley barn (page 32), the lonely farmhouse in Hazelmere (page 39) and Ymir Hotel (page 60) near Salmo are presented as splendid, if mute, monuments to a heroic and turbulent history. False fronts at Ashcroft (page 66) or the Locheil Community Hall (page 78) seem to have lingered too long and, like Gothic ruins, cling to life in a harsh, uncaring landscape. There are also fading fretwork splendours: the town house in Ladner (page 101) and the Skookumchuck church (page 125), whose gaunt, elongated forms pass silent judgment on pioneer exuberance.

This collection is about the commonplaces of our architectural history, ordinary buildings which patterned the lives of ordinary people. In his art Rudi Dangelmaier makes the mundane monumental, the ephemeral permanent. These works are an update of those of our first pioneer artists, noting the marks of human intervention in the years between—but also commenting on their brevity.

Martin Segger is director of the Maltwood Art Museum and Gallery at the University of Victoria, where he lectures in the Fine Arts Department. He is the author of *Walking Tour of Old Town Victoria, City of Victoria Conservation Report, This Old House, The British Columbia Parliament Buildings* and *The Buildings of Samuel Maclure.*

Talking Walls
Howard White

Acton Kilby, whose old general store in Harrison Mills is depicted on the cover, deserves a special place in the history of BC heritage conservation—as its mascot if not its patron saint. Old Acton, whose family ran the Kilby Store for better than half of this century, was a packrat. What he had come to possess by the sweat of his brow he wouldn't part with easily. He had the old way of placing value on things; he thought of what he'd paid for them in the first place, and how modern and proud they'd once made him feel. As for the notion a thing's value was only what you could get for it today, he'd have no truck with it. He applied this stubborn appraisal to the rusty old cream separators and broken ploughshares that crammed his woodshed as well as the dusty and outdated goods on the upper shelves of his store. He couldn't bring himself to put a good brass gaslamp pump or a nice silver-plated buttonhook on at half price just because nobody had asked for one in twenty years. He remembered their original usefulness and hung on. When the mills wound down and the town began to disappear around him the smart money guys told Acton he should sell out before his old store lost its value completely. Later they told him he'd waited too long and now the best thing he could do was knock the obsolete old building down and sell the land for dairy pasture.

Acton hung on. People laughed at the old guy with his store full of unopened antiques, but he didn't care. He knew what he had and he believed somebody was going to come in that door some day and just really want that buttonhook. It was just a matter of waitin' for things to pick up.

Then a funny thing happened. It was gradual at first, and Acton thought it might have been a fluke, but after a while it got so you couldn't miss it. People were coming in not to buy stuff but to look at it. They'd walk around the store sighing and smiling to themselves and saying, "Look here, Maw! How long since you seen an old buttonhook? And only twenty-five cents, too! Let's buy it and take it home to the museum!" About that time Acton had decided he wasn't going to sell that buttonhook after all. He'd found out you couldn't get those any more. The company that made them wasn't even there any more.

It would be hard to say just when it was Acton Kilby decided he was in the museum business instead of the store business because it happened little by little over about twenty years. At first he'd still sell bread and milk to the locals and just charge admission to strangers but by the end he was charging everybody to come in and look at his old stock of unsaleable goods. He dragged in some of the wife's old Indian baskets, dusted off his father's old muzzle-loader, shined up the old cream separator and filled up some of the shelves that had become bare over the years. He could see what people wanted, so he got himself a pork-pie hat and whittled up a pointed stick and shuffled back and forth behind the counter cracking corny jokes and telling stories about some of his favourite items on the shelves. In full flight he bore a vague resemblance to W.C. Fields. It really wasn't so different than he'd done for years, except now with these tourists he didn't have to worry about even keeping close to the truth. The worse he exaggerated the more they liked it. Most of his stories were terrible. He'd reach under the counter for a pretty little sewing kit with an embroidered lid and say, "In them days we always kept two kinds o' sewin' kits. This one here was for the womenfolk." Then he'd reach under and pull out a card of bachelor buttons.

"And this was for the menfolk."

Locals shook their heads and said he was rightly named because actin' was what he was born to do. But there was one part of his routine I always admired. He'd gesture toward the back wall with all its curling old photos and pre-war calendars and dried-up harness parts hanging from spikes and intone in his best Fields rasp, "Have you ever heard people say they wished the walls could talk? Well, the walls of this old store are a regular gossip!" Then he'd lean on a loose board in the V-joint and it would let out the most eloquent series of squeaks.

Acton is a good ten years in his grave as I write this, but his old store goes on telling its vivid story of pioneer days in the Fraser Valley to thousands of visitors every year. It is now a provincial museum and attendants with piping young voices strut back and forth behind the counter actin' out his old routine—although I'm told nobody else has ever been able to get the walls to talk quite like he could.

If heritage conservationists owe much of their material to packrats like Acton Kilby, we owe the author and illustrator of this book, Rudi Dangelmaier, an even more particular debt. It is his imaginative premise that the walls of some of our most humble and taken-for-granted buildings can be made to speak, and speak eloquently, of pioneer times.

This book is timely, because the vein of our architectural heritage Dangelmaier explores, folk architecture constructed almost entirely of wood, is so vulnerable to the frailty of age. In a historical sense, the west has been both blessed and cursed by having a cheap and plentiful supply of wood for building. Wooden building was ideally suited to the quick surges and sudden turns of an economy that mainly followed the developing resource extraction industries. A Ymir or a Barkerville could be thrown up almost overnight, and abandoned just as easily. Wood, of either the stacked log or sawn board variety, also allowed the poorest and most inexperienced settler to put a tolerable roof over his family up on the Cariboo flats or down on the Fraser sloughs.

Dangelmaier shows us another virtue of wood, and that is its expressiveness. With the artist's help, these wooden walls can speak to us of an unschooled Kamloops log cabin builder's unique way of solving a common structural problem, or the nautical background of a certain Langley church builder. More particularly the wood itself shows its age, greying and veining with the passage of time almost like human flesh. It is more expressive than stone or brick, and the perceptive seeker of history can benefit from this.

The down side is that wood doesn't last. Most of the buildings captured in these pages are just cresting the hundred-year mark as the book goes to press. In another hundred years the stone citadels and brick mansions of the east will look much as they do today but it is hard to imagine that any of the west's most characteristic monuments, from pioneer churches and barns to the great Haida totems, will be anywhere to be seen. But as the poet John Keats once pointed out, there is a record that is even more permanent than stone, and that is art. This is why we owe the immigrant German artist Rudi Dangelmaier such a deep debt of gratitude, for he has preserved some of the most characteristic structures of our pioneer years in a form that will never fade as long as there are people with eyes to see—and ears to hear the eloquent wood.

Howard White began publishing the west coast journal *Raincoast Chronicles* in 1972 and founded Harbour Publishing in 1974. His published books include *Raincoast Chronicles First Five, Raincoast Chronicles Six/Ten, A Hard Man to Beat, The Men There Were Then, Spilsbury's Coast* and *The Accidental Airline.*

Pioneer Buildings

Homestead near Aldergrove, Fraser Valley

In this starter home from the 1870s, livestock, feed and people were all kept under one roof. Clearing the land provided the logs, but no mill was available to shape the timber into boards and beams. Problems had to be solved with axe and adze, hand saw and ingenuity.

In the early 1970s the house was still standing, dilapidated, empty, perched precariously on the edge of an operating gravel pit near Aldergrove in the Fraser Valley. Now it is gone.

Landry homestead on the Summerland Flats, near Summerland

This original homestead log house typifies the pioneer spirit of the men and women who over one hundred years ago settled the Okanagan Valley.

Originally the structure housed a kitchen, bedroom and living room under a thick sod roof. Next, a master bedroom was added on, and finally the children's quarters.

Dr. Irving, a well-known surgeon in the Summerland area, was born in this house.

Log selection and fitting were done with such care that in the early 1970s the old building still served as a cottage for summer guests.

Original barn of the Gattrell family homestead near Summerland

The importance for early settlers of a sound and solid barn can hardly be overestimated. More often than not the very existence of the family depended on keeping farm implements, feed and livestock well protected and out of the weather. Small wonder that the barn frequently proved to be the finest building on the farm.

Homestead farm in the Kettle Valley

The building dates from around 1880. What makes it unique is the fact that it is truly a duplex. A centre wall divides the interior into two equal and self-contained sections with the living room and one bedroom on the ground floor. Stairs led to the loft, which was probably used for storage and as sleeping quarters for the children.

Nothing is known about the original builder.

but the structure was already there, along with several others, when the father of the 1989 owner purchased the land, exactly one century before.

The oldest private house and barn in Hedley

The name of the original owner and builder of this pioneer house was Lyons. Mr. Lyons had a contract with the mine owners in Hedley to haul lime from Keremeos, a little over twenty kilometres away. In his spare time he built this home for himself.

Living quarters occupied the centre of the building. The all-important wagon was kept in the low shed on the left, horses and feed in the tall barn on the right.

Except for the board-and-batten section in the middle, Mr. Lyons used logs from his own property for construction. The barn is roofed with hand-split boards. Heavy battens cover the joints.

When Mr. Lyons married he built a new house for his wife on the same property. Mrs. Lyons was still working as postmistress in Hedley in 1972.

Trapper's cabin near Beaver Flats in the Kettle Valley

Years before the gold rush of 1858 brought thousands of fortune hunters to British Columbia, trappers had already moved into the area and established trap lines.

Bachelors most of them, they led a simple life and their needs were few. A sturdy one-room log cabin for shelter and storage, drinking water nearby and access to a Hudson's Bay Fort where the pelts could be sold were usually all they required.

The cabin, built around 1850, was still in good condition in 1972. Only the floorboards had rotted away. Today, originals like this are fast disappearing.

19

Farm Buildings

OLD FARMHOUSE IN EAST DELTA, BC

Old farmhouse in Delta

Built around 1890 by the Brown family, this was a typical example of a well-to-do homesteader's dream, a solid, functional house in the style of the times.

Inside there were a large kitchen, a living room, a parlour, a dining room and four bedrooms. A summer kitchen and a vegetable storage room are later additions. The hired hands lived in the small house between the buggy shed and the main building. Their quarters were usually referred to as the men's house. Partly visible behind the men's house stands a large barn.

The original homestead had 160 acres of land. This has been reduced to half and at the time of publication the farm was used as a feed lot for beef cattle. The house is gone.

Chinese vegetable gardens

One by one, the Chinese vegetable gardens near the City of Vancouver are disappearing. In 1968 the one below was located on the Musqueam Indian Reserve south of Southwest Marine Drive.

Expert and diligent gardeners, the Chinese were quick to utilize the rich soil of the Fraser delta, finding a ready market for their produce in the growing city. They were out in the fields from dawn to dusk every day of the week.

In sharp contrast to their beautifully kept gardens, the houses they lived in at the time were little better than shacks. ▼

In 1973 this garden and dwelling were located near the northwest corner of Sea Island. A few years later not a trace was left. ▶

Fraser Valley barn on Lulu Island, Richmond

There are many theories about the development of these practical, functional and aesthetically very pleasing buildings, sometimes called cathedral barns. The first examples were constructed from logs and hand-hewn timbers. As sawmills began to produce boards and beams, professional carpenters took over and built the Fraser Valley barn from milled material.

It is possible that, as the farmer became more prosperous and his livestock increased, he employed the lean-to method as the most economical way to add more space to the original rectangular barn. Once this had proven practical, other barns were built in the same manner right from the beginning, and a unique architectural design for a barn evolved.

Two dairy barns with silos

These barns are located in the lower Fraser Valley on 64th Street and Crescent Island Road in Delta. Construction dates back to 1890.

The roofs and capping of the silos are quite unusual and interesting. The climbing space can be seen on the left-hand silo. It housed a ladder that reached all the way to the top. The barn with the darker roof is the older of the two. The roof is shingled and the walls are of board-and-batten construction.

From 1900 until about 1945, dairy farming in the Fraser Valley, although hard work, was a profitable enterprise. Modern methods and increased land prices have brought about many changes. As a result, old-style dairy barns like these have become obsolete. Most of the barns that still remain are used for storage while seed and feed are grown on the surrounding land.

23

OLD·DAIRY·BARNS·&·SILOS·ON·OLIVER·RD.
EAST·DELTA·B.C.

Barns and silos on Oliver Road in East Delta

These buildings were almost a hundred years old when pen and watercolour captured them in 1974. No railroad divided the land when this large dairy farm was built.

The three barns show an interesting architectural development which led to the unique Fraser Valley barn. First, the original building in the rear, simple and rectangular; next, the one on the right, where lean-to wings were added later; and finally, the barn on the left, where the lateral structures were incorporated from the beginning.

A single roof covers both silos, a feature that no doubt saved the owner a lot of money during construction.

Modern farming techniques have made these silos obsolete and they were torn down some years ago. Only the barns remain and, in keeping with the times, they were covered with aluminum roofs.

Robert McDonald farmhouse on Sea Island, Richmond

When the three brothers McDonald came from Scotland in 1864 to look for farmland in British Columbia, they settled on Sea Island in the delta of the Fraser River. As the house shows, their choice was a wise one. Hard work and fertile soil quickly repaid their investment.

More than a hundred years later, the building in its park-like setting was still one of the most impressive structures on the island. Part of the house was still occupied when these paintings were done. By the mid-1980s it had disappeared.

Robert McDonald farmhouse on Sea Island, Richmond

Hugh McDonald farmhouse on Sea Island, Richmond

This is another example of the success that could be achieved by early settlers. In the mid-seventies the house stood deserted on the farm, having long ago been replaced by a modern home closer to the road.

In recent years the land became part of the runway system of Vancouver International Airport.

**Hugh McDonald farmhouse on Sea
Island, Richmond**

28

Homestead farm, Ladner Flats

This homestead farm was demolished in 1961 to make room for a row of duplexes. The descendants of the original settler were not interested in working the land and sold it to a developer. The timber used for construction was as sound on the day it was destroyed as on the day it was built. The house used to stand south of the Ladner Trunk Road, about one and a half miles east of the town of Ladner.

With its tall windows, make-believe balcony and gable ornament the house is typical of the late Victorian period. The men's house on the right probably was a later addition.

Of interest is the square silo, one of the earliest of its type. Later, silos became more sophisticated structures.

Feed, straw, cattle and horses were all kept in the big barn, which also had space for farm machinery.

Farmhouse near Delta

The first homestead on the site was built in 1866 by a man named Asburry. Ten years later this bigger and more elaborate house replaced the original structure. Building materials were floated to the site on a slough that led to Mud Bay.

Mr. Asburry sold his farm to Christopher Hough, who in turn sold to Mr. Samuel Chorlton in 1927. In 1943, J. Erskine acquired the farm and his son, T. Erskine, finally sold out to the present owner.

The pretty house is well maintained. It has eight large rooms and a kitchen. The garage to the right was formerly the room for the hired hands.

Farmhouse on Westham Island in the Fraser River delta

The silt carried to the Pacific by the Fraser River has formed many islands. The municipality of Richmond covers most of the largest one—Lulu Island, named in 1862 after a young actress, Miss Lulu Sweet. Vancouver International Airport occupies Sea Island, second in size. Westham Island, the third largest, has so far escaped industrialization and looks much like it did after it was first settled. It was named after Westham in Sussex, England.

The farmhouse depicted stands at the intersection of Westham Island Road and Martin Road. Around 1880, when it was built, no bridge connected the island with the town of Ladner.

The early settlers built their homes either close to the river or near one of the many creeks and canals that cut into the land. People, livestock and building materials all had to be brought from the mainland by boat or scow. In order to escape spring flooding, dykes had to be constructed, marked by the line of trees in the distance.

By the late 1980s a young family lived in the house and the building was in good repair.

31

Fraser Valley barn

Developed before the turn of the century, this barn is a good example of a unique type that can be found throughout the Fraser Valley. It is distinct in design, layout and construction.

Basically, a rectangular centre section was divided by a through passage which separated the stalls for horses and calves and left room for a hayloft above. Cows were kept in the lean-to sections. Some of these barns had lean-to additions on all four sides when much livestock had to be housed.

The weight-bearing upright walls rested on foundations of fieldstone. Large beams supported the centre section. In earlier barns, the wings were additions. After the type had fully evolved, the lean-to became an integral part of the entire structure, even though it was usually built of lighter material.

The modern dairy farmer, if he has inherited one of these oldies, uses it only for storage. This particular barn stood near Highway 99 and the Colebrook Great Northern station at 131st Street in Delta.

Fraser Valley barn with silo, Delta

There is no doubt that the original owner was a well-to-do dairy farmer. He must have been progressive, as indicated by the very early silo and the stock barn at the extreme left of the picture.

Mr. Manning, the present owner of the property, now lives in Kamloops. He installed modern dairy equipment after he bought the farm from Mr. Pybus.

In the mid-seventies the building, as shown, served as a storage barn. Later it was modified and is now no longer recognizable.

1886. OLD FARMHOUSE ON CANOE PASS LADNER B.C. 66

Old farmhouse near Canoe Pass

River Road leads west out of Ladner, and near the end is a narrow stretch of water known as Canoe Pass, which separates Westham Island from the mainland. The water is too shallow for navigation. It is said to have been used during the gold rush of 1858 by miners hoping to elude the naval patrols on the river.

The lovely old Victorian house used to stand near the end of River Road. In 1974 it had long ceased to be a residence and farm animals were walking in and out of the lower quarters. But the construction and ornamentation, the fruit trees and Lombardy poplars surrounding it indicated that the original owner was well-to-do and took great pride in his home.

A few months after the sketch had been done the house was torn down.

ESTHAM·ISLAND·
HOMESTEAD·FARM·

Westham Island homestead farm, near Ladner

This house stood near Canoe Pass, the narrow waterway that separates Westham Island from the mainland. Since no bridge existed in the 1860s, settlers built their homes close to the water in order to have access to transportation.

To protect the island from seasonal flooding, dykes had to be built. In addition, a system of canals was dug to carry off drainage water. Travel and shipping of goods to the mainland had to be done by boat or flat-bottomed barge.

Today, a bridge and roads make modern traffic possible, but the island has retained much of its early unruffled charm.

House with tower, Surrey Flats

Like much of the low-lying Fraser delta, the Surrey Flats suffered from annual spring flooding until the government began to build dykes around 1890. The house belongs to this period in the history of British Columbia. Timber for the building was logged from the site and hauled to a Fort Langley mill. The style and concept indicate that the original owner had some very definite ideas about the design and appearance of his home.

The building, known as the Collishaw House, is beautifully maintained—soft beige with white trim. Surrounded by tall trees, it has remained an oasis of elegance.

Original farm home of Mr. and Mrs. Granville Morgan, Summerland

Mr. Morgan, an English immigrant, became a fruit farmer in the Okanagan. Around 1890, he built this fine example of a family home and surrounded it with an English garden.

While the house is not pretentious, the choice of design, overall dimensions and setting express a subtle feeling of pride.

Farmhouse of the Weaver Family, South Delta

Until 1945 this turn-of-the-century building was the hub of a large dairy farm. It was built by the Weaver family on the original homestead site.

The sketch shows the house from the rear, the southern exposure. The front faces what is now Highway 10. Off to the right stands the ubiquitous Fraser Valley barn.

The main house contained five bedrooms upstairs. The parlour, dining room, kitchen and utility room were on the main floor. The hired help lived in the men's house, which projects out from the main building and features a type of mud room at its entrance.

The basement was elaborate and very roomy because the house was built higher off the ground than is usual for dwellings of the period.

By 1978 the old home had fallen into such a state of disrepair that it had to be demolished. A grassy field now covers the site. By the spring of 1989, only the crumbling barn remained.

Homestead farmhouse in the Hazelmere area

Built in 1884, this was the typical house of a homesteader who was prospering on 160 acres of rich farmland.

The large barn housed a herd of sixty to seventy cows, the young livestock and a few horses.

In April of 1972 this farm had been divided and an immigrant from Poland, Mr. W.R. Rutkowski, was using seventy acres as pasture for fattening his cattle.

Like many farmhouses in the Fraser Valley, this one has a men's house, no doubt added on at a later date. The door shown leads into the kitchen. The men's quarters are upstairs.

OLD·RANGE·HOUSE·WITH·WATER·TOWER.

Old range house with water tower near Alta Lake

The hill country of coastal British Columbia, with its abundant grazing areas, was used to good advantage by horse breeders. Before 1930, the logging industry and farms provided a ready market for the animals.

Range areas were not ranches in the true sense of the word. Usually only one person was required to look after the herd for most of the year and to help with the roundup.

Water for the animals was often scarce, particularly in rocky regions and during long, hot summers. For emergencies it was stored in a water tower and allowed to flow into troughs when needed. The wooden troughs were several hundred feet long and many horses could drink at the same time. The structure for the tower is still standing but the tank is long gone.

This old range house in the Alta Lake-Whistler area is of simple lock-joint construction. The small building on the left was the saddle and tack house. In the wintertime, a sleigh was used to transport feed.

In the 1970s the house was still occupied by Mr. B. Rogers, who was quite content to live by himself with only his dog for companionship.

Doukhobor farm compound near Grand Forks

The Granby River joins the Kettle River at Grand Forks in the Kootenays, in southeastern British Columbia. Much of the surrounding area is suitable for farming and was settled by a Russian religious sect, the Doukhobors, around 1895. Strong ethnic and religious ties kept these large family groups together. They chose their new land with care and, being hard workers, their communal enterprises soon prospered.

The first small houses were constructed from wood. For later buildings they baked their own bricks. The brick building on the right, behind the root cellar, housed a steam bath as well as a spacious kitchen where fruits and berries were preserved for sale.

Younger members of the communal family lived in the large central brick house. The first floor held the living and dining rooms. Their sleeping quarters were upstairs.

By the mid-seventies this compound, about six miles west of Grand Forks, was deserted. The barns were empty. Birds and small animals lived in the houses. Viewed from a distance it looked very romantic, but close up it was a most depressing sight.

Farmhouse at Agassiz

This beautiful farmhouse was built in 1890, the proud possession of Mr. and Mrs. C. Smith.

No doubt the Smiths appreciated the social amenities of their day. It is easy to picture Mrs. Smith having a tea party for the ladies of the nearby Anglican Church—tea served on the lovely old porch under the stately beech and chestnut trees.

Once the flower beds must have produced a profusion of colours. The English love of gardening is still evident in the overgrown beds.

Fruit trees of all kinds and a herb garden to the rear bear silent witness to the fact that the original owners were learned farmers of the old country type.

In 1972 the house stood old and tired, dreaming away in the shade of the trees. In recent years it was modernized—white aluminum siding and a roof of green duroid shingles have given it a new lease on life. The porch is gone, but the beautiful old trees still remain.

Burr Villa on Crescent Island, Delta

This beautiful house is typical of a period which dictated that wealth must be shown by lavish exterior elaboration and architectural detail—an example of a stately Victorian farm residence.

Several prosperous farmers once lived in this part of the Fraser delta. Since the land was rich and needed little clearing before it could be put into production, wealth was accumulated quickly. Speculation in real estate offered another opportunity to grow rich, and the alert farmer was quick to take advantage of this opportunity.

As a heritage building, the impressive old home has been moved to Dease Island Park and completely restored. It no longer leans to one side.

The park is open to the public from May to September.

Burr Villa coach house and barn, Delta

The men who looked after the horses at Burr Villa Farm had their living quarters upstairs in the front section of the coach house.

A large room downstairs held pegs along the walls for storage of harnesses, saddles and leather goods. The better coaches and sleighs were kept well sheltered. Working vehicles had their place on the side of the barn under a roof, while horses were stabled in the building seen on the left in the picture.

A windstorm destroyed the structure in the early 1970s.

The Story of Burr Villa

as told to the artist by Mrs. Anniemay Burr in September of 1970.

It all began with William Henry Burr, who lived from 1860 to 1923. In his day he was better known as Harry. He was born in Victoria in April 1860, son of William Henry Burr, BA, and Sarah, MA, formerly of Dublin, Ireland, who arrived in Delta in the early seventies. The couple owned eight hundred acres south of Crescent Island Slough.

The Burr family had left their ancestral castle in Ireland well before 1855 and settled in Ontario. Much of present-day Toronto was built on property they owned.

When the British government asked them to establish a school at Port Douglas in 1858 they left Ontario and sailed around Cape Horn to Victoria. Mr. Burr taught at Craigflower School and later became the first teacher at Fort Langley. He found time to write a textbook on arithmetic which was published and used for some time in New York schools.

Mr. Burr Senior speculated heavily in real estate and held property valued in the millions of dollars. He owned much of New Westminster and part of Port Moody, the former terminal of the Canadian Pacific Railway.

His son "Harry" was educated in Victoria. After clerking in New Westminster he took up farming in 1889. He held title to a section of reclaimed land on Crescent Island in Delta. The property extended south from the Fraser River to Macdonald Road and was bordered by Crescent Island Road and 62nd Street.

The farm was a mixed operation. Grain was grown, hay, fruit for the canneries. Harry also raised cattle, sheep and Clydesdale horses. The products of his farm were transported on the Fraser River in steamers that called on his wharf on their way to New Westminster and Nanaimo.

The farm was known and registered as Burr Villa. It housed the first and only post office on Crescent Island.

Harry had two brothers, Joseph and John J., and a half-brother, Percy R. His sister Maria married Mr. David Price. His sister Susan became Mrs. Cowper and lived in Victoria to her one hundredth year.

In 1889 Harry Burr married Edith Blanche Mitchell, the daughter of a Delta pioneer

Original house barn near 108 Mile House on the Cariboo Highway

family. Their son, Albert Edward Burr, was born in 1901 and lived his entire life at Burr Villa, taking over after his father's death.

Albert Edward Burr married Anniemay Smith of Ladner. They had five children, Harry, Madeleine, Sylvia, Bernadine and Terry. All grew up at Burr Villa and were educated in the Delta area.

Albert Edward Burr died in 1969. In 1970 his widow, Anniemay, was living alone at Burr Villa. The old wharf on the Fraser was gone and the land was no longer farmed.

In 1870, in the Cariboo, it was not uncommon for a family to own six to ten horses for personal transportation only. The animals were kept in a house barn, the garage of the period.

Frequently, the exchange horses for the stage coach were stabled here as well. The ranch hands had separate quarters for their horses.

Ranch and roadhouse near Mile 108, Cariboo Highway

By the mid-1870s, stagecoaches and freight wagons provided a regular service along the Cariboo Highway. The distances covered in a day were not great by today's standards—about fifteen miles for freight and perhaps twice that for the stagecoach. Thus, roadhouses to provide rest, food and shelter for man and beast became important and it wasn't long before they could be found spaced along the rough trail.

Generally, the family homes of the ranchers served as rest stops. Facilities to accommodate travellers and animals were added.

The front part of the building in the picture was originally the ranch house. The section extending to the rear served as hostel for the guests.

Rarely did these friendly places have their own names. Instead of *Shady Rest* or *Henry's Lodge* they were simply called after the number on the nearest milepost, hence 100 Mile House.

Community Buildings

Harrison Mills general store

Built in 1860, this complex was still a going concern when the Kilby family took it over in 1912. Store, hotel, post office, butcher and blacksmith's shops were all busy. When it was first built, it was called Manchester House.

For years the Harrison Mills general store provided the last opportunity for men on their way to the Cariboo gold fields to sleep in a decent bed, to receive mail and wait for spare parts.

The entire complex has now become Kilby Provincial Historic Park and the old store serves as a museum. It stands at the confluence of the Harrison and Fraser Rivers and the CPR main line runs in front of the store.

The store was set on stilts because the unbridled Fraser flooded the low-lying area every spring. The big flood of 1948 did some damage to the structure, but this was repaired.

As the gold rush petered out, the district of Harrison Mills was settled and became a beautiful area, dotted with dairy farms.

Old stores in Ladner

This row of houses used to form part of the main street in the little town of Ladner on the lower Fraser River. In the old days, when life was a little slower, a ferry connected Ladner with Lulu Island. It was only natural that the street leading to the ferry dock would become a busy commercial thoroughfare.

In time there came better roads and a tunnel was built. The leisurely ferry disappeared and Ladner's main street lost its former importance.

A beautification committee in 1972 concluded that the old houses had to make room for modern buildings, and you will find them no more. At time of publication only the long, low building on the right remained. It had been updated and contained a food store.

Courthouse at Yale

Built around 1900, this was actually the third Courthouse in Yale. The other two burnt down and were never rebuilt.

The house is located close to the old Anglican church above the CPR tracks, near the site where Yale's railway station once stood.

The house was a private residence and in good repair when this picture was painted.

EARLY·FAIRGROUND·BUILDING·LADNER·B.C.
71.

Delta Agricultural Hall, Ladner

In the 1890s, when this building was erected, the fairgrounds lay on the fringe of the actual townsite, in the country so to speak. Over the years Ladner spread out, and in 1971 the proud building with the prominent flagpole found itself surrounded by modern homes and streets.

If clapboard walls could talk, they would no doubt have spoken of festive and patriotic occasions when large crowds streamed through the double doors to view things grown, raised or manufactured in the community.

A wide stairway led to a second floor that held a number of dividing walls of unknown purpose.

In the rear of the building was a spacious kitchen that must have played an important role in keeping visitors happy.

Today this venerable structure has become part of Deas Island Regional Park, where it stands near Burr Villa.

Railway station hotel, Fort Langley

For a hotel the location in 1890 was ideal, as travellers merely had to step across the railroad tracks to find good food and accommodation at Fort Langley, the first seat of government in British Columbia. There must have been many a noteworthy guest in those days and it would be interesting to browse through the old hotel register.

The hotel was built to last, with heavy timbers, a solid plaster coating and cedar shakes on the roof.

The picture was painted in 1971. A year later the building had been completely revamped and turned into a beer parlour with cocktail lounge and restaurant. Although most of the original hotel was incorporated into the new building, it no longer resembles the original structure, which was an unusual mixture of English Windsor style and utilitarian New World practicality.

Front Street, Harrison Mills

In 1870 Mr. G.W. Beach owned the shingle mill and provided housing for some of his workers and their families. The second-last house in the picture served as an office and engineer's residence, while the mill owner lived in the house on the extreme left. These two were the oldest buildings on Front Street.

In all there were twelve residences on the site, with a mess hall and kitchen for the single men shown on the extreme right.

The mill ceased operation in 1948. Two years later the last man moved away. By the mid-seventies all buildings were in a state of collapse. Vandals had demolished most of the furniture, removed fixtures and broken every window.

By 1989 not a trace remained of the buildings on Front Street.

Miner's Hall and Opera House, Rossland

In 1898 the Miner's Union of Rossland, one of the first in Canada, needed a meeting place. At the same time the mushrooming town was looking for a community hall, a centre for social activities. The many Welsh miners and their families in particular wanted a hall for cultural events and a place to keep their traditional choir alive. Wisely, the town's people decided to build one hall for all their needs.

The large building features five floor levels. It houses a stage and many dressing rooms. For years it was rented regularly to travelling opera companies. At time of publication a theatre group was using the building and continuing the rich tradition of the past.

Nearly a hundred years later the imposing and impressive structure, now known as the Rossland Opera House, still attracts the attention of anyone travelling through Rossland. It has become a Provincial Heritage building.

ST·JOHN·THE·DIVIN
MAPLE·RIDGE

St. John the Divine Anglican Church, Maple Ridge

The Royal Engineers built this church in 1859, when they were called in by the governor to survey a road into the interior. British Columbia was still a territory and the mad rush of gold seekers digging their way up the Fraser River showed no sign of letting up.

The pretty little church was moved to a site on River Road in the heart of the Maple Ridge community, where it was still being used in 1989. It had a resident clergyman and was well attended, seating about seventy people.

The structure is characteristic for the time it was built, all wood, with clapboard siding and shakes on the roof. It was well preserved and had a sanctuary and a small add-on sacristy.

Princess Margaret and other members of the royal family have attended services here.

OLD·METHODIST·CHURCH
LADNER, B.C.

The old Methodist church in Ladner

This building served the Methodists in Ladner from about 1880 until the 1930s, when it was still packed for Sunday services and there was "powerful singing going on." It survived a move from a few blocks away to its new location in a lane.

In the 1970s it was used for paper storage by the *Ladner Optimist*, a local newspaper. Later it was demolished.

Anglican church in Yale

Dedicated to St.John the Divine and built by the Royal Engineers in 1868, this little church has seen a lot of history.

Yale used to be the head of navigation on the Fraser river, and had a shocking reputation during the gold rush of 1858. It was a place where gamblers and miners rubbed shoulders with prospectors, painted ladies and promoters of every stripe. Later the new road through the Fraser Canyon brought more people and the CPR used the town as a construction depot.

At one time the little church stood just above the hustle and bustle of the streets running close to the river boat landing.

In 1972 the streets were deserted and few people bothered to stop at Yale. The town had lost its purpose and was dying. However, the little Anglican church looked strong enough to ride out many more years.

Old blacksmith's shop, Greenwood

The reasons why this little shop was still standing after nearly a century are obvious. First, the builder used rocks for his creation and second, it stood somewhat off the beaten track just west of Greenwood.

Of course there was no longer a blacksmith shaping horseshoes at his anvil. Instead, the solid building served out its days as a garage and storage place. ▶

54

Old hotel in Ladner

By today's standards, this small hotel looks rather insignificant. Yet a hundred years ago it was new and modern, it provided food and shelter, a room for the night and a convenient location in the centre of town close to ferry dock, livery stables and stores.

Like many other historical buildings in Ladner, it was doomed.

Grauer's general store on Sea Island

Mr. J.J. Grauer, the man who built this general store shortly after the turn of the century, was a pioneer in more ways than one. He built his new store almost entirely with concrete, one of the first buildings of its kind in British Columbia.

The store was strategically located in the neighbourhood of Eburne at the foot of the Marpole bridge, which no longer exists. The only other store at the time was about seven miles away to the south, in Steveston.

In 1972 the store was still owned by the Grauer family and operated by Lester and Clay Grauer. The second storey apartments were occupied and the old building was flanked by the former residence of R.M. Grauer, the old Eburne post office and Burns' Meat Market. In time these buildings had to make room for progress.

Hall and general store in Agassiz

During the pioneer days of British Columbia, shelter was at a premium and many buildings had to do double duty. This was such a building. Constructed in 1894 by the International Order of Odd Fellows—who still own a commemorative brick—the main floor housed a general store and a butcher shop. Separate stairs led to the upper storey, which was used as a lodge and community hall for meetings, parties and dances.

New owners purchased the building in 1967 and twenty years later they were still operating a buy-and-sell business on the main floor while using the upstairs as living quarters.

The old drill hall in Armstrong

It was a sign of the times that even the smallest of cities had to have a drill hall, a place for the military to practise. The Canadian Army used these halls until the end of World War II for the training of reserve units.

The drill hall in the picture was built at the turn of the century and handed over for use by civilians after the last great war.

By 1972 the sign showing the regimental affiliations had been painted over and the new sign above the main entrance proudly proclaimed the building to be the Centennial Hall. It was used for exhibitions, fairs, and for indoor sports.

Christ Church, Hope

There is something about the general style of these early Anglican churches in British Columbia that makes them identifiable even to the casual passerby. Perhaps it has to do with the fact that they were designed and built by the Royal Engineers, a 165-man detachment of public works specialists brought out to assist the colony during the gold rush period.

Historians differ on the exact date of construction of Christ Church in Hope, a Hudson's Bay post, but indications are it was built in 1866, two years before the Anglican church in Yale. At the time the Royal Engineers were surveying the Dewdney Trunk Road, which runs east through the mountains along the border between British Columbia and the United States.

The small building on the left is a church hall, still being used in 1989, as was the church. The City of Hope has converted the adjoining area into a park, which gives the old buildings a most charming setting.

Ymir Hotel, Salmo Valley

Ymir, in the east Kootenays of British Columbia, was a shipping centre and not a mining town in the strict sense of the word, but it catered to several mining operations in the nearby hills and depended on the ups and downs of stock markets far away.

In the 1890s, when Ymir was booming, it supported four hotels. In 1984 only this one was still operating. Perhaps it was the beer parlour, behind the addition on the ground floor, that kept it going. ◄

Original pub in Greenwood

Like many towns and villages in British Columbia, Greenwood, west of Grand Forks, exists because there was a mine. Rarely was it possible for the mine owners to recruit local labour. In 1890, when the pub was built, British Columbia was still in the process of being settled and the population base was small.

Miners and sawmill workers came from everywhere. Many were of Chinese origin, many were transients, pursuing one dream or another, merely stopping over for a time.

In order to keep the peace among the motley crowd, the authorities tried racial segregation. The building in the foreground was reserved for whites only, the building behind it was reserved for the Chinese and the farthest building, of which only part is visible, was the local flophouse, kept aside for transients and others of dubious character. ▲

Lodge, International Order of Odd Fellows, Ashcroft

Protective legislation of the kind found in British Columbia today did not exist when this lodge was built in 1890. In order to spread the burden of sudden hardship and care for its members, service organizations like the IOOF were formed and attracted many people. Their meeting places, the lodges, could be found throughout British Columbia.

Ashcroft was no exception. Judging by the size of the building, the IOOF must have had many members. The lower floor housed the offices of the chapter and the living quarters for the caretaker, while the hall occupied the second floor.

Modern social services legislation reduced the need for the volunteer charity of these valuable associations and many of their lodges stand empty today.

In the mid-seventies this building in Ashcroft was occupied by an undertaker and an ambulance service.

Old hotel, Rossland

Two big fires around the turn of the century destroyed most of the buildings along Columbia Street, Rossland's main street, but this unique structure escaped. In 1898 it shows up on the assessment rolls of the town of Rossland as the War Eagle Hotel, one of five such establishments in the bustling community. The owners at the time were Messrs. Van Ness & Walker.

In recent years the building was covered with stucco and the window shapes were changed slightly. Otherwise it has remained essentially the same. At the time of printing it was owned by Mrs. Velma Gipman and served as an apartment block.

Original town hall, Ashcroft

Unlike Europe, where the landscape was dotted with cities, towns and villages long before the iron horse was invented, many settlements in British Columbia began as strategic points along the railroad tracks. Although started as a roadhouse on the Cariboo Road, the town of Ashcroft came into its own as a service point on the CPR.

The settlement quickly developed into a small town with schools, churches, stores and hotels. In 1880 the city hall was built and, not much later, the community hall, seen behind it.

The Prince Charles Hotel, Ymir

Originally the hotel was built and owned by a couple from the southern United States. This may account for the imposing architectural style, which does not blend well with a location named after Ymir, the frost giant of Norse mythology.

What intrigued the artist was not the ornate balcony system but the fact that the columns are unevenly spaced. After some time pondering the mystery, it was discovered that they had been placed in this manner to take advantage of natural fieldstone footings. Whoever the unsung architect was, he didn't mind spoiling the symmetry of his design to save the expense of constructing new footings.

In its boisterous heyday, around 1890, the Prince Charles was one of four hotels in Ymir and catered only to the best customers. It boasted the finest bar, a pool room, a card room and a legendary dining room with exquisite food and courteous service.

And then the town died. The rails were torn up. People moved away. Still standing in the 1980s, the once glamorous Prince Charles sheltered only memories of a glorious and exuberant past. ▶

Old Chinatown, Ashcroft

Old Chinatown, Ashcroft

It is not possible to separate the history of Ashcroft on the Thompson River from the history of the Chinese people in British Columbia. They helped lay the tracks for both railways, the CPR and the CNR.

Many Chinese settled in the area around Ashcroft and began to farm the land. They brought their produce into town for shipping. Chinese merchants built stores in Ashcroft to provide their countrymen with goods and foodstuffs most familiar to them. The stores became centres for social contact as well.

As long as the Chinese farmers patronized the stores the merchants prospered. This happy situation changed when Canada began to import farm products from the USA. Unable to compete, most Chinese farmers left the area and many merchants soon followed.

Fifteen years ago only a few remained, hanging on to their stores, trying to do business as before. Unfortunately, their efforts failed and by 1989 the last vestiges of Ashcroft's Chinatown had disappeared.

Old stores along Railway Street, Ashcroft

These stores were built around 1880, nine years after British Columbia entered Confederation and only a hundred years after Captain Cook stepped ashore at Nootka on the west coast of Vancouver Island.

Towns like Ashcroft developed almost overnight. Demand for goods and services was quickly followed by supply. The stores along Railway Street, parallel to the tracks, were built and owned by Chinese and Europeans. A hundred years later, the old buildings were being demolished to make room for supermarkets.

Original Anglican church at Barkerville

Much has been written about the old mining town of Barkerville, tucked away in the mountains east of Quesnel. In 1862 it briefly held the world spotlight as headquarters of the great Cariboo gold rush. Then it fell into oblivion for a century, to re-emerge as a provincial heritage site and a popular destination for tourists.

Fortunately many of the original buildings were left undisturbed by the town's hundred-year slumber, including this church, which was built around 1865.

The picture shows the exterior of the sanctuary as well as the addition, which was soon needed to provide room for the growing congregation.

Original sporting house, Barkerville

As in all mining towns of the young crown colony, the early population in Barkerville was predominantly male, and most of the males were bachelors. It did not take long for the ladies of easy virtue to follow the trail of the gold seekers and offer assistance, should it be required, in the dissipation of fortunes large and small.

The saloons did big business, and so did the sporting houses. Usually the latter buildings were located near the outskirts of town.

The picture shows a house of simple log construction with a board-and-batten front and a wooden boardwalk where the men could shake the mud off their boots. The entrance structure sheltered waiting clients from the weather. Credentials were presented through the little window in the front door before admittance was granted.

Constructed around 1865, the humble log house tells of a practical society that solved obvious problems without hypocrisy.

Livery stable and blacksmith's shop, Ashcroft

Yesteryear's car rental agency was the livery stable, a place where horses and buggies could be rented. Usually they were located near hotels, stores and railway stations.

This rather well-preserved example in Ashcroft, built around 1890, also housed a blacksmith's shop where horses could be shoed and farm machinery repaired.

As motorized vehicles became popular, the garage to the left was added around 1905. Three quarters of a century later the building was still in use, serving as a storage facility for lumber.

Old Presbyterian church, Ashcroft

This church was built around 1890 and most of the work was done by volunteers. Neither the builder nor his helpers had much training in structural engineering, architecture or design. Everybody contributed to the best of his ability and knowledge. The result was a lovely building in what we today call the pioneer style.

Like so many old buildings, this one was judged to be standing in the way of progress and was demolished. ▶

The original bank in Armstrong

The Bank of Hamilton operated from this building for fifteen years before it was purchased by the Bank of Montreal. Instead of using the building, however, the new owners built a modern bank near the railroad tracks.

Constructed entirely of wood around the turn of the century, the building has a colourful history. At one time or another it housed a hotel and bar, a casino, a bake shop, a bank and various stores. When the picture was painted, the upper storey had been converted into real estate and insurance offices. The second-storey verandah still bore the playing card symbols of a less dignified past.

74

St. Alban's Anglican Church, Ashcroft

This is the oldest church in Ashcroft. It was built in 1885, soon after the community had grown to a size that could support a church and a pastor.

Except for the modern addition, the building is virtually unchanged from the day when the original contractor turned the completed structure over to the parish—for the grand sum of one thousand dollars! The price covered all labour and material but it did not include the bell.

Original firehall, Ashcroft

Fire is a constant danger in a town where virtually every house is built of wood. The job of watching over Ashcroft was carried out by dedicated volunteers who got their firehall in 1890. The building was used to store equipment and for training. The tower protected the hoses when they were hung out to dry and was topped by a bell which called the men to duty. The low part of the structure housed the all-important pump, a manual affair that required four strong men to operate it.

St. Luke's Anglican Church, Vancouver

This pretty little church was formerly located on Southeast Marine Drive near Fraser Street in Vancouver. The obvious English influence in style and construction of these early missionary churches was rarely copied by assemblies of a different religious persuasion.

Today the trees are gone, and so is the church. Industrial buildings occupy the site.

Community store, Ruskin

The English philosopher John Ruskin was honoured in the naming of this small Fraser Valley town, not for his erudite critiques of Renaissance art but rather for his thoughts on the co-op movement, which were admired by the founders of the local Canadian Co-operatives Society sawmill in 1898. The mill, alas, proved no credit to its namesake, plunging into bankruptcy the very next year, but the community store in the village carried on, proudly bearing Ruskin's name for another century.

In pioneer days people exchanged news at the store. Government announcements, auctions and social events were posted on the notice board. The bench on the porch was a comfortable place to linger in the summertime, and when the snow whirled around the windows, people crowded around the wood stove inside.

The CPR station was not far, and fishermen on the Fraser River below had only a few steps to walk for a loaf of bread.

The community store at Ruskin was still active in 1971, but by 1986 termites and rot had damaged the structure beyond repair and it was torn down. The site is now vacant.

The two original schoolhouses on Westham Island

The older building is the one on the right. It dates back to 1880 and was located near the east side of the island. In 1900 it was moved to become an addition to the new schoolhouse, where it was used as a playroom.

Both buildings were demolished in 1970.

Lochiel Community Hall, North Bluff Road, near Langley

Built around 1901, the hall was still being used for weddings and local dances as late as 1972. Now it has been torn down. Inside it held a stage, a kitchen with a water pump and a wood stove, and several back rooms that may have been used as dressing rooms or for card games.

For an added touch of elegance quite out of keeping with the period, the hall was equipped with two privies.

Port Guichon, Ladner

Port Guichon is a few years older than the town of Ladner. The picture shows the old hotel and police station, in 1961 the only remaining buildings of the old port. In 1860, immigrants, gold seekers and adventurers waited here to board the river boat for the 150-mile passage upstream to Yale.

Port Guichon was the terminus of the Great Northern Railway. After the CPR bridge across the Fraser River in New Westminster was completed and a ferry dock was built in Ladner,

Port Guichon silted up and died. In time it was absorbed by the growing community of Ladner. The buildings are no more.

Firehall at Moyie

Moyie shares the fate of many small towns in the British Columbia Kootenays. First there was the dream. Then came the mine, and with it the workers and their families. A sawmill was needed, houses were built and became homes. Homes had to be protected, so in 1907 they built a real firehall in Moyie with a tower and a bell, with space for pumps and hoses and a large room in the back where people could sit and talk when there were no fires to be fought.

And then the dream faded. The mine closed. The sawmill fell silent. One by one families moved away and left behind the mountains and the lake, their homes and their firehall.

Sunbury School, River Road, Delta

Finnish and Norwegian fishermen established the community of Sunbury on the banks of the lower Fraser River. In 1891 they built a two-classroom school for their children. As the population grew, two more rooms had to be added in 1902.

In 1946 a new school was constructed to the east of the old building and the original schoolhouse was boarded up. It has not been used since that time.

Sacred Heart Roman Catholic Mission Church, O'Keefe Ranch, near Vernon

Like all circuit churches, this one did not have a resident priest. Rather, a travelling pastor would arrive once or twice a month either on horseback or with horse and buggy, doing his circuit. He slept and cooked in a small room adjoining the church proper.

Instruction, distribution of the sacraments, weddings, baptisms and burials were usually attended to before Sunday Mass.

Close to the church is a cemetery with tombstones, some of which were over a hundred years old when this picture was painted in 1960.

Sharon United Church, Murrayville

The little settlement of Murrayville in the Fraser Valley is named after the Murray brothers, who came from Scotland. In 1890 they owned large tracts of land close to the border between Canada and the United States.

The Great Northern Railway had surveyed a line to connect Bellingham, Washington, with Vancouver, BC, leading through much of the property owned by the Murray brothers. They speculated that a small town and a railroad station on their land would suit them very well indeed. A site was laid out and promotion began.

Yet for one reason or another, Murrayville never really got off the ground. Little of the dream remains today but some interesting old buildings, among them this church, which dates back to 1890. It was remodelled in 1976; a hall was added, the front reconstructed, and a black duroid roof replaced the old cedar shakes. Little evidence of the old sylvan setting has remained.

St. George's Anglican Church, Fort Langley

Dedicated to the patron saint of England, this quaint little church stands at 9160 Church Street in the old residential area of the town of Fort Langley. The outside of the original building, centre, shows the style of most early pioneer structures. But the little cupola that houses the bell and the flying supports for the roof overhangs give it an individuality that makes it unique.

The carved mouldings and the care with which material for important doors was chosen impart an almost nautical air, as if a shipwright had a hand in the construction. Stained glass windows mellow the light and create a feeling of composure and dignity inside. The nave seats about sixty parishioners.

The church was built in 1901 near the Hudson's Bay Pioneer Cemetery and is still in use. The bell tower had to be replaced in 1982.

St. Alban's (Otter) Anglican Mission Church

St. Alban's Anglican Church, near Aldergrove

This little mission church is dedicated to St. Alban. It was built in 1890, dismantled in 1926 and then reconstructed on the southeast corner of the intersection of 246th Street and Fraser Highway between Langley and Aldergrove.

When the church was first built it belonged to the Langley circuit and was located at Milner, a small community about halfway between Langley and Fort Langley. After it was moved it became part of the Aldergrove circuit.

The building is of wood construction with clapboard exterior walls, a feature typical of construction methods at the time.

By 1989 the ancient structure had been reborn as a daycare centre.

COMMUNITY. STORE
ALBION. B.C.

Ritchie's General Store, Albion

The store was located at the corner of Lougheed Highway and 240th Street in the municipality of Maple Ridge. When it was constructed, Albion went by the name of East Haney, and the two roads crossing here were called Baker and River.

There was no store when Mr. and Mrs. Ritchie moved into the house seen in the background in 1870. Their son John built the general store in 1901 and it was operated by the family until 1954.

Any general store that operates for half a century at the same location becomes part of the landscape, a man-made monument whose usefulness goes well beyond the mere selling of pepper and salt, cloth, yarn, lard, carbide for the lantern and charcoal for the flatiron. Of necessity it becomes a social centre as well. How many specialty shops does it take today, how many private and government agencies, to carry out the many functions of a single general store in a small community?

OLD STORE AT WOODWARD'S LAND...

Store at Woodward's Landing, Richmond

For many years the only link between Vancouver and the Ladner, Delta and Point Roberts areas was a government ferry that crossed the south arm of the Fraser River between Woodward's Landing on Lulu Island and Ladner to the south. Traffic was always heavy between those points and long lineups at both approaches were quite common.

Built in 1885 and situated at the south end of Number 4 Road in Richmond, the store sat strategically near the ferry dock. Ice-cream cones and other goodies relieved the monotony of the wait. Children especially loved the quaint little store.

The ferry stopped running when the Deas Island Tunnel—now the Vincent Massey Tunnel—finally connected Delta with Richmond.

OLD·FAMILY·HOME·
AT·SURREY·CENTRE·ON·OLD·MCLELLAND·RD·B.C.

The Boothroyd house, Surrey Centre

This solid-looking house is situated on the corner of Old McLellan Road and 60th Street west of Cloverdale. In 1885, when it was built, it had room for a large family. The outside walls consist of heavy overlapping siding, a type of construction reminiscent of the New England states in the United States. It is very likely that the original owner or builder brought the style and design with him when he settled in the area.

In the spring of 1989 the ancient building was surrounded by a large, park-like lot. A porch had been added to the house. New siding covered the exterior walls and the old maple still towered over the building. Even the bare-branched pear tree was blooming.

Christ Church, Surrey Centre

Since 1885, Christ Church has been sitting on a hilltop overlooking the flats of Surrey. The Anglican church is surrounded by a cemetery and some of the old gravestones date back to the middle of the last century.

The wooden structure has great architectural appeal. In 1971 the clapboard siding was painted a soft grey trimmed with white. Everything was well tended and Sunday services were conducted regularly.

In 1980 Christ Church was designated a Heritage Site. ▶

Grocery store, Hazelmere

The community of Hazelmere once supported three stores, a church and a community hall. The building shown dates from 1895 and was the only store left when the painting was done in 1971.

The store underwent several alterations after it was first built, but the general layout was not altered. Its old-fashioned charm was much enhanced by the lovely surroundings. Today this store no longer exists.

LIVERY STABLE & BLACKSMITH SHOP.

Livery stable and blacksmith's shop, Ladner

Jordan's Livery Stable was erected in 1881. The location was very convenient, only a few steps from the ferry dock at the north end of town and within easy walking distance of Ladner's main street with its shops and stores.

The lofty sign has been painted over and Delta Furniture acquired the building in 1947. At time of publication it was on Delta municipality's Heritage Advisory list.

Early schoolhouse, Harrison Mills

In the last century, it was usual for the teacher of a one-room school to find room and board at a nearby farm. But not in Harrison Mills. Here the teacher's residence and schoolhouse were combined. School began in earnest in 1884, when the new building was finished. It is said that a daughter of the founder of Woodward's Stores taught school here in 1900.

As the population outgrew the building, it was acquired by the Kilby family and moved to its present site. The interior was altered to make it suitable for family living. The government of BC now owns the old schoolhouse as well as the adjoining store, to which it is connected by a walking bridge. Both are designated Heritage Buildings.

ITY·HALL·HAZELMERE·B.C.

Community hall at Hazelmere

The social life of the early pioneers centred around this meeting place. Horses could be left in the barn, while buggies would be parked in the open space to the left. The women were busy preparing meals in the large basement kitchen.

Once this was a happy place, important, active, full of life. But by the mid-seventies vandals had smashed the windows and destroyed most of the interior without the slightest regard for former generations who had worked and paid for this building. Now it is gone.

Henry Hope's blacksmith shop, Armstrong

At one time the town of Armstrong easily kept three blacksmith's shops busy, a fact that underscores the importance of this highly respected trade for early settlers. In 1972 Henry Hope's shop was the last one left and Mr. Hope, though well into his eighties, was still working at his trade. He had bought the shop from the original owner in 1905. The building dates from 1890.

With Mr. Hope's passing the era of the village blacksmith, anvils ringing and horseshoes hissing in the cooling trough as children gawk in the doorway, is no more.

Knob Hill School, near Armstrong

Many oldtimers in the Armstrong area had the three Rs drummed into them in this one-room school. It was the second one in the neighbourhood. The first school stood about two miles distant and was closed when this one was built around 1890.

At first the school was financed entirely by the local settlers, but eventually it became part of the School District of Armstrong, the smallest one in the Province of British Columbia. The average attendance here was between twenty and twenty-five students.

It was a solid building from the start. The top structure rests on log sleepers and these in turn rest on fieldstone corners. The addition on the right held the wood that fed the potbellied stove inside. Two outhouses complete the arrangement.

Classes ceased in this building in 1918, but it has continued to serve the community as a church and hall.

Bandstand, Phoenix

Phoenix, in the "border country" south of Greenwood, was one of the province's larger mining towns in the 1890s. Today the only traces left standing are some fragments of the powerhouse walls. Everything else has been bulldozed.

Happily, some perceptive soul saved the old bandstand and moved it to Greenwood, where it can be found on a hillside not far from the main street. It is now a heritage building.

This quaint little structure from the past shows that even in the most frantic turn-of-the-century boomtown people were interested in things other than making money and mining ore. To the painter it seemed a hopeful sign, bearing witness to the irrepressibility of man's impulse toward the arts.

Pioneer Anglican Church, Ymir

This little Anglican church in Ymir was dedicated to St. Francis. It was built around 1885. Construction was simple and entirely in keeping with the precepts of its patron saint, who called poverty his bride. It had room for about thirty-five people. A small addition, left, took care of Sunday school. Services were last held in 1950 and were attended by two families.

Twenty years later, when the picture was painted, the building stood rather forlorn on level ground at what may once have been the centre of the now deserted town of Ymir. The roof was leaking, the floor was decaying and the benches looked rather rickety. Only the small altar and the cross on the gable betrayed the fact that at one time this building had been a church.

Pioneer District School, Mile 140, Cariboo Highway

It becomes more and more difficult to find one of these old fonts of knowledge in British Columbia.

They are no longer needed. They serve no useful purpose. They get in the way, as old things will do.

In 1973 this old school house stood undisturbed in a field off the old Cariboo Road, which is snaking its way along the contours of the hillside in the background. The structure was still in fair shape but the two privies were falling apart.

The simple log structure, built in 1880, is a good example of early pioneer schools, when all grades sat in the same room and the teacher boarded with a rancher nearby. Note the stile to the left, built so that children could safely cross the fence. A gate would not have been practical—range cattle could wander into the schoolyard if someone forgot to close it.

Sullivan's Store, Sullivan's Corner, Surrey

The Sullivan brothers were early pioneers in the lower mainland. One of them operated a sawmill and the other one built and operated this store, which was located on the corner of Johnson Road and 64th Avenue in Surrey.

The lower floor held the post office, the general store and an office for the justice of the peace. Upstairs was a community hall for dances, political meetings and group gatherings.

The former BC Electric Railway from New Westminster to Chilliwack passed close by, and in 1922 the first train stopped at Sullivan's Corner, a gala event that called for a big celebration. The tracks are hidden behind the white fence in the picture.

Passenger service ceased long ago, and today only the occasional freight train rolls past the site.

After serving the community for well over seventy years Sullivan's Store burned down in the winter of 1972.

Fraser Valley grocery store, Port Douglas

The architectural structure indicates that this little store was first built around 1900. It was strategically located about one mile north of the Douglas border crossing—at the time the only point where the international border could be traversed between British Columbia and the state of Washington.

It appears that the owner did a little farming on the side. The old gasoline pumps tell their own story of changing modes of transportation.

The sign on the left side of the roof advertises the hotel near the border crossing.

The old store was demolished in 1986 to make room for the widening of the intersection of 176th Street and 8th Avenue.

99

Fine Homes

TOWNHOUSE.
AT. LADNER. B.C.

Town house in Ladner

This beautiful home belonged to Mr. McNeely, who owned and operated one of the first general stores in Ladner. Obviously he prospered and was proud to show it. Mr. McNeely paid the grandiose sum of three thousand dollars to have his house built.

In the early seventies it was still in good condition, though sitting sadly out of context in the middle of a new bungalow development. The property, at 3900 Arthur Drive, has recently been given to the Catholic Church. ▶

Town house in Ladner

The type of construction and materials used place this house well into the Victorian era, before the end of the last century. It was built for Mr. Cornell, one of the early settlers in the Ladner region.

On the south side an octagonal solarium gives the appearance of a small chapel. The porch faces east and the gable wall faces north.

Still occupied in 1989, it has been beautifully refurbished and received a well-deserved Heritage Merit Award. The lovely old building stands at 4847 Georgia Street. ▶

H.N.R. Rich residence, Ladner

Mr. Rich, who was said to be the third white child born in the Fraser delta, had this house built in 1889 at a cost of a thousand dollars.

In 1971, when the picture was painted, the stately house sold for ninety thousand dollars. The grounds were well kept and university students were using the building as a boarding house. In the early 1980s it was demolished to make room for an apartment building—Ladner
◀ Manor, at 4926 48th Avenue.

Town house, Vernon

The mansard roof with dormer windows, the elaborate fret ornamentation on the frieze below the roof and the elegant bay windows all express distinction and pride of ownership in this fine family home. Located at 22nd Avenue and Schubert Street, the house commands an excellent view of the countryside.

The posts by the entrance and the trellis below the overhang appear to be the only major changes to the original building. Everything else is typical of a family town house built in the year 1900.

102

Town house in Greenwood

Millionaires were not uncommon in the mining towns of the Kootenays at the turn of the century. Many of them preferred to live in the community where they had their business.

Greenwood boasted quite a few residents that belonged to this wealthy group and many of their fine old homes are still standing.

It was not enough to merely have money. Wealth had to be exhibited, or so the people believed at the time. Location of the house in the better part of town was important. And certain architectural features simply had to be incorporated in the structure to make it respectable. A tower was always good, several porches, bay windows, balconies, all this surrounded by lawn, shrubbery, cultivated trees and flower gardens, separated from the less fortunate by a wall topped with a wrought-iron fence.

The house shown was built in 1889. When the original owner left, it fell into disrepair. In the early 1970s a new owner gave this magnificent old house a new lease on life.

Town house in Ashcroft

In 1885, when this pretty little house was built, a town house was something only the well-to-do could afford. It was essentially a winter home that enabled people to partake of the *season*, winter being a time for concerts, the theatre and other social activities that a larger settlement offered. In the spring the whole family moved back to the ranch.

The crown on the roof was called the captain's walk or widow's walk, an idea borrowed from the New England states.

Old town house in Fort Langley

Fort Langley was the first seat of government in British Columbia. The Hudson's Bay fort, located near the Fraser River, was the nucleus of the first settlement. As farmers began to cultivate the surrounding land it was only natural that a townsite should develop. Merchants, professionals and artisans set up their businesses and shops.

This house stood at the corner of Mavis Avenue and Clover Crescent. It was a typical style of the period around 1870. Bay window and front entrance were roofed over. Ornamental face boards and other purely decorative frills spoke eloquently of an original owner with means. A well-treed garden completed and complemented the charming setting.

In 1973 this grand old lady had been replaced by a concrete structure.

Old family home, Vernon

This type of roof structure originated in France and came to British Columbia with settlers from Quebec. It is called mansard after the architect who invented it, Francois Mansard.

A house of this design is eminently practical for large families since the attic area can be partitioned off into bedrooms.

The bay windows are typical of the turn of the century, when this house was built. Walls rest on a foundation of fieldstone and concrete and were plastered at a later date. Originally this house had clapboard walls.

Indian Reserve Buildings

Indian reserve church, Harrison Mills

In the spring of 1970, only three houses on the Indian reserve were still being used as residences. The pretty little church that had lasted a hundred years was already a mere shell. Vandals had been at work smashing windows and tearing up boards.

When the picture was painted, in 1956, an ancient cannon stood near the entrance to the church, a gift from the Hudson's Bay Company. The old field-piece had been used to chase away marauding coastal Indians who came up the Fraser River in their canoes to steal young women.

Not appreciating its historical value, some-one recently sold the venerable gun to a private collector from the prairies.

Indian reserve church, Tsawwassen

Blacktop covers the former site of this lovely little church, as the highway leading to the Tsawwassen ferry dock runs over it.

The church was built around 1880 and served the needs of the Indian population on the reserve for many years. During the 1950s the Augustinian Fathers from the monastery in Ladner still held services here.

Indian reserve church, Musqueam Reserve, Vancouver

One of the earliest pictures in this collection, it was painted in 1942 and shows the original church, which is now long gone. At the time Chief Jack Stogan lived in the house on the far left, William Guerin in the middle and Edward Sparrow closest to the church.

The building reflects the influence and encouragement of the young French Oblate missionaries who worked here. It is reminiscent of much older churches in northern France.

Like many mission churches, it had no proper foundation and was built on cedar blocks. When the cedar decayed, the steeples fell, one by one.

Indian reserve church, Laidlaw

A building that has lasted more than seventy years has earned the right to be called old. Yet compared with churches more than twenty-five years younger this turn-of-the-century mission church near Laidlaw looks comparatively modern.

The wood construction was conventional, walls made of clapboard belted at top, bottom and corners. Shingles cover the roof.

The Oblate Fathers from Hope still held services here in 1971, but these were discontinued a year later.

Looking for a Church

"There is no church here, mister." The young Indian stood his ground, a barely perceptible touch of defiance in his dark brown eyes.

"But—I drove for two hours to find your reserve. I have it on good authority that there is a church here, a real pioneer church, you know, one of the very early missionary churches. It's supposed to be very beautiful. I came here to paint a picture . . ."

"Yeah, well." He looked down and gently kicked a clump of tall yellow grass, then looked up again. "Sorry about that, mister. We don't know of any church here."

Abruptly he turned and shambled away, shaking his head a few times as he walked.

Two mostly black mongrels watched from under an old blue Ford on blocks. All four wheels were missing. The reserve simmered in the hot sun of early afternoon; houses widely spaced, an overturned tricycle on the lawn, a celluloid doll without arms sitting on a fence post. And no sign of the church I had come to paint.

"Car trouble?" The voice shook me out of my beginning disappointment.

"No, the car is fine." I turned and beheld an elderly gentleman.

"If it's the car, Henry can fix it." His thumb indicated a turquoise house with a red roof. "Henry's good at fixing cars."

"It's not the car," I said. "I came here to paint a church. Now there's no church here."

"I know," he said. "That's because of the mudslide, see?"

"You mean the church was destroyed by a mudslide?"

"You could say that," he cackled happily. "The slide got the train, and that started it all." He stared at me as if everything had been explained already, waiting for me to join in his laughter. "It was hopper cars, see? From 'lberta. Grain, you understand?"

I didn't.

Sadly he shook his head. "All that fine grain all over the tracks. Well I tell you, Henry was out there in no time with buckets and a shovel, and so were the others. We got a lot of grain that night." He nodded with obvious satisfaction. "An awful lot of grain."

"And?"

"Well, we took it all into the church, piled it up right in front of the altar. The Fathers haven't been around in years. It was quite a pile, I tell you." He raised his hand well over his head and nodded. "Quite a pile."

"You mean—"

"That Henry, he's good with machines. He fixes cars and everything. His dad was good with cars too. It's in the family, you see? Lawnmowers, chain saws, everything. So, Henry figures we've got it made with that free grain and all. He welds up a boiler and copper tubing and all that, and then he builds a still."

"In the church?"

"Where else? That's where all the grain was, didn't I tell you? Right next to the grain he builds a fine still, a real good-looking machine, and the tubes go up and down like this." His hands weaved patterns in the air. "And we had a bathtub for the booze, see? With lion's feet, one of them real oldies with lion's feet."

"And then?"

"Well, I tell you." He swallowed and nodded. A shadow of sadness swept over his face. His kind old eyes fixed on a cloud castle faraway. "The whole kit'n caboodle blew up, the church, the still, the grain and everything. There was a bit of a fire too." After a time he said, "You sure there's nothing wrong with your car? Henry can fix it . . ."

Indian reserve church, Popkum

While no one knows the exact date when this church was built and dedicated to St. Maria Magdalene, it can safely be placed between 1875 and 1885. The method of construction and style indicate this period.

Surrounded by old cherry trees, this architectural gem sleeps on a hillock overlooking the Fraser River. No services have been held here since the early fifties. Most of the Indians who still live on the reserve have their homes in the western section, while the old church stands in the eastern part. It is merely a shell now, without windows or doors. The cross that topped the steeple is already gone. In a short time the wonderful, soaring structure will become no more than a memory.

Last smokehouse on the Musqueam Indian Reserve, Vancouver

The name *smokehouse* was bestowed on these buildings by white people who rarely got a chance to look inside. For the Indians this was a *long house* or *big house*. It belonged to a family clan with a dozen or more members. Ceremonial fires were kept burning inside and smoke emerged from the house all day long, hence the misunderstanding.

The one shown was built around 1865 near the north arm of the Fraser River, where the Musqueams had their village. The house on the extreme right was owned by Cyrus Point, whose family also at one time had a *big house*. ▲

111

Indian reserve church, Katzie, near Hammond

British Columbia is rarely visited by hurricanes, but in 1962 Hurricane Frieda wreaked havoc in the Lower Mainland. It toppled trees in Vancouver's Stanley Park and truncated the spire of this little church on the Fraser River nearly thirty miles to the east.

At one time more than 150 people lived on the Katzie Reserve. Over the years the population dwindled and the church fell into disrepair. The last person to celebrate mass here was Father Clarke, who came from the Oblate Fathers' school for Indian children in Mission.

Indian reserve church, Sea Bird Island, Agassiz

In 1956, when the painting was done, the little church was leaning a little. The cedar stump foundations had rotted away and no effort had been made to replace them.

Yet the church was neat and tidy inside. The scent of fresh flowers hung in the still air. Shafts of amber and red slanted from the stained glass windows and even the harmonium was in good order.

An elderly Indian woman by the name of Mary cared for the church as she had cared for people. Besides her own, she had raised several foster children. They all took training in nursing or hairdressing, and one young man attended the University of British Columbia.

The church has long since been replaced. ▶

ST. FRANCIS XAVIER CHURCH COQUITLAM RESERVE

Indian reserve church, Coquitlam

This very beautiful church has been gone for
many years. It was built in 1880 on the banks
of a small stream that flowed down to the
Fraser River.

In 1940 there were still two dozen families
living on the reserve, but by 1970 only one
house remained and the church with its three
spires had been torn down.

114

ECHELT. B.C.
MICHAEL'S.CHURCH

Indian reserve church, Sechelt

Though the Sunshine Coast is part of the mainland, it is only accessible by ferry. The Sechelt Indian Band lands straddle the narrow isthmus between the Strait of Georgia and Sechelt inlet. The location and setting of both the band lands and the village of Sechelt are very beautiful.

Particularly impressive is the Indian cemetery on the hillside. Strange iron crosses mark graves that date back to the turn of the century.

The graceful neo-gothic church was built around 1885. Unfortunately it burnt to the ground in 1971.

115

Sacred Heart Church

Indian reserve church, Semiahmoo, White Rock

From more than a hundred families, the population of the Semiahmoo Indian reserve had dwindled to only twelve by the year 1953. Still, mass was celebrated every other week in this appealing little church which dates back to 1889. The first grave was dug in the adjoining cemetery in 1892.

The church had room for about one hundred parishioners. A high altar was flanked by two smaller ones and the bell rope led from the chubby tower down to the entrance.

The reserve died gradually as more and more families moved away. When his congregation had shrunk to one regular attendant, the priest from Mission stayed home.

At the time of writing the empty church was not being kept up; nor had it been vandalized. But—a large new carving shed had sprung up right behind it, where a sixteen-foot cedar log was being transformed into a totem pole. ▶

Church of the Holy Redeemer, McMillan Island, near Fort Langley

This little church stands on an island in the Fraser River opposite Fort Langley. It was built between 1897 and 1902 and regular services were still being held there at time of writing. In 1962 the original wooden steeple was replaced by an aluminum structure. The house in front of the building has since been demolished.

The island was named after James McMillan of the Hudson's Bay Company, the founder of Fort Langley. ▶

Indian reserve church near Chilliwack

The name of this church is Sacred Heart. It was built in 1880 on the reserve of the Skwah Indian Band along the Fraser River by the Oblate Fathers, who were very active at the time. They had a pronounced influence on the style and design of many missionary churches.

The church burnt down in 1965 and was ◀ never rebuilt.

Vincent Pierre's home, Mount Currie

The house of Vincent Pierre was built by his grandfather around 1885. Somehow, Grandfather never got around to sawing off the projecting ends of the lap-joint construction.

The house rests on cedar foundations. It holds two rooms and a kitchen downstairs and two bedrooms upstairs.

Vincent himself reshingled the roof a few years before the painting was made. He left the scaffolding in place in case it was ever needed again.

When Vincent Pierre passed away, the house was moved to the back of a lot and became a storage shed.

VINCENT·PIERRE'S·HOUSE.

OLD·INDIAN·RESERVATION·HOUSE.

Log house, Mount Currie

Benedict Sam's grandfather built this house with great skill and meticulous care around 1890. The lap-joint corners are neat and exact and the adze-squared timbers were fitted so well that no chinking was required. Heavy cedar bark shingles cover the roof.

Originally the house held three rooms and an attic. Later a kitchen was added on.

The house is still standing on the Mount Currie Indian reserve. Benedict Sam has since passed away. He lived here when the painting was made, but he didn't own the house.

ARNOLD·RITCHIE'S·HOUSE. OLD·RESERVATION·HOUSE

The house of Arnold Ritchie, Mount Currie

The cedar logs for this house were squared with an adze and neatly dovetailed at the corners. This time-consuming method paid off in the long run, since the walls could not move. The hand-split shakes of the roof rest on peeled poles. No paint was ever used on the outside. The wood was allowed to weather, which over a century resulted in a soft and mellow appearance. A few horses and cows were kept in the outbuilding behind the house.

In 1971, when the picture was painted, Arnold Ritchie attended university in order to become an anthropologist. He supported himself by selling Indian artifacts. He has since moved away.

The house was vacant for a time. It is as solid as ever. At time of writing the Nelson family owned it.

St. Paul's Church, Capilano Indian Reserve, North Vancouver

The ambitions and the pride of the Coast Salish Indians are embodied in the architectural dimensions of this Catholic church. The mission was founded in 1880 and the church was built four years later. It must have been quite a showpiece in the early years—a beautiful church near the water in Vancouver's inner harbour, with the lovely North Shore mountains for a backdrop.

The house on the left is the rectory. The parish was under the direction of the Oblate Fathers and the church was blessed by Bishop Durieu, who was also an Oblate.

In 1981 St. Paul's became a National Historic Site and underwent extensive repairs and restoration. These were completed in time for the Squamish Indian Band to celebrate the church's hundredth anniversary. ▶

Indian reserve church, Cornwall, near Ashcroft

When Clement Francis Cornwall arrived from England to raise cattle near Ashcroft, one of his first concerns was to find ranch hands for his large spread. He turned to the local Indians for help and they became his source of manpower.

To show his appreciation, Mr. Cornwall founded the only private Indian reserve in British Columbia. In 1863 this little log church was constructed on the reserve and dedicated to St. George, patron saint of England.

The Indians on the Cornwall reserve are very proud of their little church. At last word, services were still being held every second Sunday. ▶

Indian reserve church, Yale

This little church is dedicated to St. Anselm, who was archbishop at Canterbury almost a thousand years ago. The church was built in 1894 under the supervision of the Oblate Fathers. Irish, English and American elements can be seen in the architectural style.

In the mid-seventies the church was still serviced regularly by the Oblate Fathers from Hope. Since there is no separate Roman Catholic church at Yale, both Indians and ◀ whites attended services here.

House of Chief Mark We-get, Kitselas

Halfway between Hazelton and Terrace along Highway 16, which connects Prince George and Prince Rupert, is the reserve of the Kitsell Indians. They have a language all their own and once were a large tribe, but in 1974 only about a hundred people remained.

Around the turn of the century their Chief was Mark We-Get. For reasons that have not come down to us the chief thought it important to own a real white man's house. So he began to build one. He copied the tower and flagpole, long double porch, windows and doors, and he constructed his house in the shape of an L.

And then the money ran out, or Chief We-Get lost interest, or both, and the house was never finished. Since his death, around 1930, no one has lived in the building.

The totem pole was an outstanding example of Tsimshian carving.

Indian reserve church, Fort St. James

In the last century, Fort St. James was a prominent Hudson's Bay post. Valuable furs were collected from Indians and white trappers and shipped down to the coast along a route that was known as the Anderson Trail.

The picture shows two of the oldest churches in British Columbia. They were built between 1865 and 1870. The original Roman Catholic Church is the little log building on the right. It was later replaced by the much more impressive structure in the centre.

Both churches were built under the guidance of the French Oblate Fathers.

Sacred Heart Church, near Katz

Katz was a railway stop about twelve miles west of Hope, and Sacred Heart church can be found on the Chawathil Indian reservation on the north side of the Fraser River.

The pretty little church, built around 1900, used to serve several Indian reservations. It is dedicated to the Sacred Heart, and the Oblate Fathers from Hope look after the spiritual needs of the parishioners.

At the time of writing, services were still ◄ being held once every month.

Holy Cross Church, Skookumchuck

The Skookumchuck Indian reserve is tucked away between high mountain ridges near the south end of the Lillooet River and Lillooet Lake, about thirty-five miles from Mount Currie. It is a remote and very pretty reserve, ideally located near excellent fishing and hunting grounds.

The church shown is unique in that it boasts three spires of the neo-gothic type. It was built around 1880 by Indian artisans under the guidance of the Oblate Fathers. French influence is noticeable in style and execution.

The building rests on heavy cedar logs which have been sunk into the ground. Hand-adzed sleepers support the floor.

In recent years the church was restored and Father Bob Haggarty of Mount Currie began holding services here once every month. ►

Industrial Buildings

Original powder house, Rossland

Considerable blasting was required when a railroad was built to the mine near Rossland. The explosives were stored in powder houses located in the hills away from the city.

The one shown dates from 1895.

Powder houses were built in special locations. The spot had to be shaped like a large funnel. Should the explosives blow up accidentally, the blast could only go straight up and ◀ not do much damage.

To further minimize danger, the heavy log structure was covered over with planks and animal skins which in turn were covered with a layer of sand and small rocks. A layer of topsoil completed the work and soon grasses and bushes grew on the roof.

Inside, a powder house held shelves for the boxes of explosives. The door was built solidly from two-inch planking and only the foreman had a key to the padlock.

Pioneer Granite Works, Fraser River North Arm.

Granite was quarried in the Nelson Island area north of Pender Harbour, then barged to Vancouver to be remanufactured. Many city buildings rest on granite foundations. Blocks were also shipped to the prairies to be cut into gravestones. This plant operated from 1905 until 1940. Increasing use of concrete and a change in architectural tastes forced the owner to close down. ▲

Old sawmill, Ruskin

The mill in the picture produced cedar shingles. It was built around 1890. Less than a generation ago there were many mills like this one still operating on the banks of the Fraser River. Their burners sent plumes of smoke into the sky and occasionally a shower of sparks escaped from the wire cage—quite a spectacle on a dark and windy night.

Logs were transported cheaply on the water.

The employees lived in the neighbourhood. They could walk to work and home again. There was a feeling of satisfaction, of having done a day's work, of local prosperity. Most of this disappeared when the mills stopped running and the age of the commuter dawned in the Fraser Valley.

Making a Picture

A landscape painter is an oddity who doesn't quite belong. Sitting there with his easel and brushes he sticks out like a sore thumb. He attracts attention. People want to know what he's doing. Some are a bit shy, and careful not to disturb his concentration. Others walk right up and ask.

"What are you doing?"

"I am painting a picture."

"That's the old shingle mill you're making a picture of, right?"

I nodded. It was the old shingle mill I had roughed out. The man now stood beside me and watched for a while, his sharp old eyes darting from paper to building and back. He looked like he had lived in these parts all his life. Perhaps he had even worked in the mill before it closed down.

"You know," he said kindly, "it'll take you a long time to make a good picture. Maybe all morning."

"Yes."

"Tell you what," he said after a few minutes. "Seems to me, you aren't getting things right. The roof isn't as crooked as you've made it. And the door sits more to the left, not much, mind you, just..." He was groping for words, trying to be helpful without offending. His mouth opened, then closed again as he thought some more.

"It must be awfully hard to get an accurate picture of things as they are," he finally concluded. "Now my brother, you see, he's got a box. All you have to do is look through a little window, and you can see everything in that window just as it is out there. All you have to do then is press a little button and out comes an accurate picture. Takes no time at all. Matter of fact, I'm going to get it for you right now!"

Old blacksmith's shop, Milner

In 1971, this was the only shop remaining in the entire Fraser Valley that operated solely as a smithy. Mr. Moir, the owner, was then eighty-two years of age, but he was still shoeing horses four or five hours every day.

He and his brother had come from Scotland to Canada in 1890 and the shop dates from 1895. The walls of the building were of board-and-batten construction, a method now rarely used.

Tractors and mechanized farm implements have replaced the horse and yesteryear's simpler equipment. Mr. Moir has passed away, and so has his shop.

HATZIC VALLEY, B.C.
CAMERON SAWMILL

Fishing settlement, South Delta

Dozens of small fishing settlements dotted the banks of the lower Fraser River, the sloughs, the creeks, the tributaries, from the beginning of the century. Houses floated on platforms made from logs, as did net lofts and marine repair shops. Small canneries were built on pilings, their loading docks reaching out into the tidal water.

In later years the fishing industry began to concentrate around areas like Steveston and the picturesque old sloughs were allowed to ◀ crumble and wither away.

Cameron sawmill, Hatzic Valley

Many small sawmills operated in the Fraser Valley around the turn of the century. Most of them have disappeared, as timber rights, and the small mills that owned them, were purchased by bigger forest product companies.

The Cameron mill was located at the far end of the Hatzic Valley. Mission was the nearest town.

The mill was started by Mr. and Mrs. Cameron, who came from Scotland. When market conditions were good they employed up to twenty-five men in their small operation.

In the 1950s they sold out and retired to live out their lives in the lovely and familiar Hatzic Valley. ▲

Dormitory buildings, Old Summerland

Apples, apricots and cherries will rot on the tree if they are not picked in time. The work is seasonal. Pickers and cannery workers are desperately needed for a few months, and then they move on.

The picture shows the quarters provided by the canneries in Old Summerland for their seasonal workers. The buildings date from 1915 and resemble army barracks in their unadorned functionality. The local residents never liked them. Nor did they welcome the seasonal workers or accept them into their social life.

The buildings housed mainly women, who came from Indian reserves and Doukhobor settlements. No recreational facilities were provided for them. Small wonder that social problems developed. In the end the cannery owners had to close down the buildings.

BC Pea Growers Ltd. elevators, Armstrong

Where it develops, industry will put its distinctive stamp on any landscape. A fishing village cannot be mistaken for a farming community or a logging camp.

These storage elevators attest to the activity of pea growers in the area. They form such a prominent part of Armstrong that they are difficult to overlook.

The smaller of the two was built in 1900, the larger one two years later. The walls are of wood siding and rest on concrete foundations. At time of writing, both elevators were still in use.

The building in the background was a new store and stood on a site formerly known as Chinatown, a part of Armstrong that burnt to the ground in 1918.

Celtic Shipyard, Blenheim Flats, Vancouver

It is difficult for a painter to resist the magnetism of old buildings, fishing boats, water and trees, especially when age has mellowed the contours and years of weather have added their own gentle tints.

This shipyard began operation in 1889. It changed owners in 1914 and was still function-ing well into the 1980s. The template shop and the old ship's ways still function as efficiently as ever.

Not much water shows in the little canal but at high tide even a large fishing vessel could be launched or hauled out for repairs.

CELTIC SHIPYARD
VANCOUVER. B.C

Celtic Shipyard, Blenheim Flats, Vancouver

Sawmill, Harrison Mills

The shingle mill in the picture was built around 1900 by Mr. G.W. Beach to replace an even older mill that had stood on the same location. Nearly fifty people once earned wages here. The mill produced edge-grain red cedar shingles which were sold under the trade name of Keystone to United States markets.

In 1948 the mill closed due to a strike and was never reopened. The machinery stood idle and began to rust. A scrap metal dealer took most of it away.

Mrs. Ella Pretty, president of the Harrison-Agassiz Historical Society, explained that a fire in 1969 destroyed the remains of the old mill. Only the boiler was left when she visited the site in 1989.
▶

Transportation

CHEAM·VIEW·STATION

Cheam View Station, CNR main line, near Hope

In 1900 there must have been a compelling reason to build a railway station halfway between Chilliwack and Hope. Industry perhaps? A community requiring service? Whatever it was, in 1973 the charming station was torn down. It had been empty for many years.

At one time ice and coal were stored underneath the building. The double doors led to the freight storage area. The bay windows provided light for the office, and the door to the far right led to the waiting room. The agent slept in the small bedroom downstairs, while the station master had two bedrooms upstairs.

All that was left by the middle eighties were a few fruit-bearing trees.

Railway water tower, Port Mann

The picture shows the last and largest water tower in the Fraser Valley. It stood for over sixty years and was demolished in 1971.

The enormous volume of water was required because the marshalling yards at Port Mann were extensive. Many small steam locomotives worked here shunting freight cars, assembling trains for the long trip east or taking them apart for distribution in British Columbia. When diesel engines replaced steam locomotives, the tower ceased to be of practical value. ▶

Old roadhouse, Port Guichon

Today's truck stop was yesterday's roadhouse. These essential buildings were strategically located along the arterial highways of colonial British Columbia. The distance between them was geared to the speed of draft horses. Ten to fifteen miles was considered a good day's work for a team pulling heavily laden wagons.

Horses could be stabled, fed, watered and rubbed down, and for the teamsters there were hearty meals and draft beer, a place to sit and chat and get out of the weather. Bunks were provided as well.

Often the owner operated a small store on the side for the everyday needs of the local people.

Like most roadhouses in British Columbia, the one shown, built in 1865, has long since collapsed.

Old house, Silverdale

By all appearances, this building looks like a spacious and practical wayside inn. The two privies, with outside entrances away from the main doorway, support this impression. The construction method used indicates that it could have been built around 1870. Yet the present tenant was told that the house was built in 1911 as a grocery store with warehouse above.

In 1989 the old building stood on cement foundations at 29677 Lougheed Highway. The original windows had long been replaced with modern ones and, instead of cedar shingles, duroid covered the roof. The building was used as a bicycle shop and living quarters.

THE·OLD·PENITENTIARY·
FRASER·RIVER·DOCK·BLDG·

Old penitentiary dock building, New Westminster

Those who sinned against society in 1870 in British Columbia were taken by boat to this building. From here they were transferred to the main prison.

In 1972 the old holding tank had been empty for many years.

At the time of writing the property was owned by Hyack Air and used for storage. The building, at 60 East Columbia Street in New Westminster, has changed little over the years.

10·1900 SUMMER·RESORT·ON·THE·PITT·RIVER·B.C.

65.

Bridge, Pitt River

A village springs up, a town grows, a business prospers and all of a sudden there is the wish to get away from it all, to have a summer home, a cottage by the lake, a place to escape to, peace and quiet. . .

The bridge underscores this point. It used to span a creek that flows into the Pitt River not far from where it joins the Fraser. The area is scenically very beautiful and located just far enough from the hustle and bustle of Vancouver or New Westminster to provide a real change.

As early as 1900, summer cabins and weekend cottages were built along narrow paths by the river. To insure privacy and keep vehicles out, the bridges were deliberately kept narrow. Supplies had to be brought in by wheelbarrow or boat.

Today even the bridges are gone and only the water provides access to this secluded area.

140

Old logging bridge near Pemberton

After 1900, logging operations shifted from easy access to logging in increasingly mountainous territory. Horses and oxen pulled the logs one at a time over skid roads and bridges to where they could be floated down flumes and rivers, the cheapest form of transport.

The bridge shown is typical of the period. Note the ingenious method of tying together the end supports with steel cables.

Murray House, Murrayville

Roadhouses were utilitarian establishments. They were not places where the rich, the refined or the aristocratic looked for lodging and accommodation.

One of the few exceptions was this hotel in Murrayville, which Bill Murray had built some time before 1889. It tried to appeal to travellers of all classes. From Vancouver it could be reached in a day via the Old Yale Road.

A hundred years later the stately building was still standing and occupied.

Livery stable and blacksmith's shop, Rossland

Every town and village in British Columbia had a livery stable around the turn of the century. Horses could be rented here, traded, bought or sold. Fashionable buggies were available, but so were carts and drays. Visitors could leave their mounts for a day or a week when they came to town to do some shopping or socializing.

The building shown could easily put up forty horses. Buggies, saddles and harnesses were kept in the centre section. The blacksmith did his work in the back. The waiting room and the office were located to the right. The rectangular box adjoining it housed more offices, and on the far right the old firehall can be seen. All three buildings survived two big fires which destroyed much of old Rossland.

With the coming of cars and trucks the Rossland Transportation Company took over the old livery stable buildings, which probably saved them from being torn down years ago.

CPR station, Agassiz

All railway stations seem to have a certain functional practicality about them which makes them look alike, except for the name on the sign. The station at Agassiz escaped this fate and shows some individuality. It was built in 1893, before the design of stations was standardized.

The large shed on the right, a later add-on, indicates that at one time Agassiz was an important freight centre for the Kent region north of the Fraser River.

In 1985 the entire building was moved across the railroad tracks to its new location on the property of Agriculture Canada's Agassiz Research Station. A year later, with waiting room and station master's office restored, it re-opened as the Agassiz-Harrison Museum.

Railway dock and freight shed, CPR, Old Summerland

For the first quarter of the century, fruit growers along Lake Okanagan depended on stern wheelers for freight and passenger service. These quaint vessels were gradually phased out and tugboats with barges had to be brought in.

Suitable docks were built on the lake. The one shown dates from around 1905 and was operated as a freight dock until 1973.

Refrigerated trucks and an ever-expanding system of highways have since sent tug and barge the way of the paddlewheeler and left the lakefront to the recreational boater.

Timekeeper's house, Harrison Mills

"Yes, I knew that house. My son and I were in it when it burned down in 1980. We had to climb out the window!" said Mrs. McGee.

The house was built around 1890 for the timekeeper of the old Rat Portage Mill. As the mill closed down and was dismantled, the building was moved across the railroad tracks and set down on McGee's property, where it served as a family home for many years.

The McGees have since built a new house on the old site, at the corner of Kilby Road.

Ranch and roadhouse, Westwold

The stagecoach took two days to cover the distance between Vernon and Kamloops. The halfway point was this roadhouse at Westwold. Here passengers had the choice of staying overnight to catch the next day's coach, or continuing after a short rest and change of horses.

The house was well equipped to cater to the travelling public. In all there were two kitchens, eight bedrooms, several pantries and store rooms, a common room, a dining room, a summer kitchen and a large loft.

The house was built around 1880 and located on the old coach road. Only a shell remained in 1972.

Dray station, north of Grand Forks

The word *dray* originally described a vehicle without wheels, a sledge for example. Later it came to mean any vehicle for heavy loads.

During the peak of mining operations, around 1890, teams of horses pulled drays filled with lime up into the hills to the mine. They returned with loads of ore, which was taken to the railway station in Grand Forks. Forty miles of rough road had to be covered. At the dray station tired horses were exchanged for fresh teams.

Occasionally a stage coach would use the facilities, but a dray station did not usually cater to travellers. It was built and maintained by the mine.

The structure in the foreground sheltered hay and straw. A spare dray was kept under the lean-to next to the station-keeper's house. A horse stable, a smithy and a barn completed the arrangement.

The artist was startled in his search of the premises to find two dusty rooms occupied by an elderly woman hermit. She had been quietly making use of the abandoned facilities since 1922, over fifty years in all.

Roadhouse, Cariboo Highway, near Ashcroft

The original Ashcroft Manor stood about a quarter mile from this building. After it burned down in 1925, the house shown inherited the name.

This structure was built by C.F. Cornwall around 1870 from lumber produced in his own sawmill, and has served as a home and inn ever since. In 1974 the Parker family lived here, descendants of the Cornwalls, but the building was no longer used as an inn.

The style and construction reflect the Victorian period, and American influence shows in the ornamentation.

Agent's house, Colebrook Station, Delta

This house was built in 1904, a year after the Great Northern Railway track from Blaine, Washington, to Vancouver, British Columbia, was completed.

The station agent lived in the larger section to the left, the freight agent on the other side.

Colebrook Station no longer exists, but in 1972 track master Bill Porter and his family lived in the quaint and practical building, which was still owned by the Great Northern Railway.

In 1989 the house stood unchanged at the foot of Station Street. Bill Porter and his family had moved away and the new occupants leased the house from the Burlington Northern
◄ Railway.

Ranch and guest house, Mile 148, Cariboo Highway

A man named Steve Tingley operated a famous express agency out of this ranch and guest house in 1870.

The meticulous execution of the dovetail interlock on the corners of the building paid off in more than a hundred years of trouble-free service. The small house to the right is the out kitchen or summer kitchen where food was
◄ prepared for the hands during roundup time.

CPR water tower, Yahk

When steam locomotives still pulled freight trains with logs, ore, coal and lumber from the Kootenays to the coast, the machines had to be serviced and maintained at regular intervals along the line. An ample supply of fresh water was as important as coal.

The tower shown is a typical CPR type. It was built around 1895. Diesel locomotives rendered it obsolete and it was demolished. ►

Miscellaneous

Hunting cabins, Boundary Bay, Delta

These small and often quite pretty huts were
built by hunters between 1890 and 1900 and
used during duck-hunting season. Unlike the
cabins on the Point Roberts side, they were not
meant to be summer homes or weekend
cottages. All of them have long since fallen
apart.

School bridge in the Fraser Valley

School buses were not even dreamt of when these little bridges were built. Only the most fortunate enjoyed the luxury of a plodding ex-workhorse and most children walked to school. Often, swollen creeks and flooded ditches made a shortcut across the farm impossible and they had to take the long way 'round.

Farmers accommodated the children by building these little school bridges. The artist found one still standing but virtually all of these charming creations were allowed to collapse without a thought toward their uniqueness.

Telegraph station, Black Water Creek

Between 1866 and 1867 the Collins Overland Telegraph Company had visions of connecting North America and China by cable. Stations like this one, about twenty miles from Prince George, were built along the proposed route through the wilderness of central British Columbia. Unfortunately for Collins, the undersea cable was completed first and the firm abandoned the project. The buildings were allowed to collapse and none are still standing.

Old sluice bridge, Serpentine River, Surrey

The annual flooding in the delta of the lower Fraser River compelled the government to build dykes around 1900. In order to keep the area drained and the incoming tide out, sluice gates were installed to control the flow of water.

This bridge stood close to the King George Highway in Surrey. It was being used for local traffic until the early years of the Model T Ford and served anglers for years after until it passed into history.

Catalogue of paintings and drawings

Index